T0207573

THE  I'M IN

JOHN MACLENNAN

WESTBOW
PRESS®
A DIVISION OF THOMAS NELSON
& ZONDERVAN

WestBow Press books may be ordered through booksellers or by contacting:

WestBow Press
A Division of Thomas Nelson & Zondervan
1663 Liberty Drive
Bloomington, IN 47403
www.westbowpress.com
844-714-3454

ISBN: 978-1-6642-1063-9 (sc)
ISBN: 978-1-6642-1062-2 (e)

Library of Congress Control Number: 2020921373

Print information available on the last page.

WestBow Press rev. date: 01/08/2021

CONTENTS

GOD'S GUIDANCE

I would like to know You, God,
to see into Your heart.
To feel Your hand on mine
and know from where to start.

Your understanding beggars me
for You made all things new.
Before I ever came to pass,
You knew where my last breath would be.

Your light shines about us everywhere
when we breathe and when we laugh.
It triumphs over darkness deep
and leads us on into our sleep.

June 2013

THE PARADE OF YESTERDAYS

I was with you in the beginning
and will be there till time finally ends.
That will be a day to celebrate,
when I come and make all things new.

How I wish that time would come tomorrow
and fill all our hearts with glee.
To welcome You and the angels,
at last coming down here to see.

That will be a day that will end all days
and make a beginning anew.
Which leads into my new creation,
a world where all will be free.

August 2017

WHAT YOU TOLD ME

Talk to me about what you have seen,
the earth and its beauty
and all that has been.

Speak softly and sweetly
and in gentle tones.
Don't alarm me
or leave me ever alone.

What you've told me,
I'll remember
and treasure all the days of my life.
Until at last it is over and ended
and drifts gently into the time that has passed.

June 2015

A LITTLE BIT OF LIFE

I thought I saw you standing,
weeping in the rain.
Summer comes tomorrow
and will wipe away the pain.

Greet it with a blessing.
Meet it with a smile.
Shout a hallelujah;
it means you've gone another mile.

Road's end comes to meet us
laughing in the dark.
That will be a day
that lights another spark.

July 2008

UPON REFLECTION

What did you mean when you spoke to me
all those ages ago?
Was it a word without meaning?
Or was it to silently go?

I've learnt from this experience
nothing at all
for all that I knew before.
This means that your words are without meaning
except to those who know.

So hallelujah into the future,
where flowers and thistles grow.
Where we find that life has no meaning
but was only a passing show.

December 2017

WAITING A LONG ENOUGH TIME

What do I want to tell you about
since ever I was alive?
About hearing my thoughts from yesterday
and why they are still alive.

Do they produce fruit,
or are they lost in the sands of time,
where all my thoughts come from
all the way down the line.

What is the chiefest of all these thoughts
popping into my head without being summoned?
Why I am a poet at all
and not just a simple sinner?
Who knows the answer to that,
    not even I.

I am sure there's an answer to everything
if we wait a long enough time.

May 2020

THE HEART

The heart knows the reasons
that the mind cannot fathom.
God knows our hearts
and caresses them gently.

All His truth is poured out there
and there understood.
Let us stand in awe of its greatness,
guiding and leading us all of our lives.

Thank you, God, for giving us
our hearts of gold
that know and feel
all You tell us
and reach ever upward
for all that You know.

February 2015

BROKEN FRIENDSHIP

Yesterday everything happened.
Nothing was left unsaid.
What you said broke my heart in pieces
and left me alone, the undead.

Thank you for being my savior.
Thank you for being my friend.
Why must good things end in disaster
and happiness come to an end?

You taught me a little of life.
You helped me along the way.
Now you have gone forever
and left me with nothing to say.

I'll always remember our friendship
And treasure the times we had.
Thank you for making it easy.
Thank you for ending the bad.

July 2014

YESTERDAY

I thought about you yesterday,
when the sun shone in the sky.
All those days that heaven made
that have long passed by.

I hope to greet you tomorrow,
when the sun is red again.
All those days like yesterday
will come flooding back again.

Do not remember me
when I am gone.
But keep a cherished kiss
from times that were
and all the times that have gone amiss.

September 2010

THE WAY OF THE WORLD

Why is there conflict between us?
Why does one turn against another?
Exploitation and gain
are in the heart of these activities.
How to satisfy the demands of the world.

All of us are trying to find something to do
that will satisfy everyone
and even ourselves.
A mindless search
that could lead nowhere,
only heartbreak at the end of the road.

I'm trying to write poetry
but must rely on God, the source of all.
He, it is, who inspires the poet
to write words he scarcely knew made sense at all.

So thank you, Lord, for showing us the way
to turn feeble thoughts into expressions of belief;
that capture the working of everyone's minds
and turns them into
a creed without a belief.

April 2020

ABOUT A CIRCUMSTANCE
IN TIME

It was there, reaching out to us,
whispering words of regret.
Telling its story of sorrow
of all that had not happened yet.

Did it explain anything to me,
anything I wanted to hear?
Good or bad or indifferent,
or even affecting me near?

This is summer, isn't it,
when what we dream becomes true?
Even from the depths of sorrow,
a new horizon comes into view.

Just as today followed yesterday,
over and over again.
Just as tomorrow is forever,
so it is with you, my friend.

July 2019

COMING AND GOING IN TIME

In life we see many things.
Time crosses our paths irreversibly,
and what we saw never comes back.

Life is made of experiences,
good and bad and in between.
We learn the inevitability of suffering
and understand Satan's hateful schemes.

The constant revolving of time
often takes us unaware.
Too late we realize what might have been.
had we considered, it might have changed our fates.

We won't point a finger at each other
for ignoring its warning signs.
Rather, we trust in the future
and await what it will bring.

May 2015

WHY?

There are people who existed long before I.
They were there before ever I was thought of.
And they mapped out a life for themselves,
which would never be undone.

None of us know the way ahead
or what could come.
Rapture and sunshine for some,
and for others, just what remains to be done.

If we dream of a paradise
just lolling in the sun,
it is not really that.
It is wishing for a better tomorrow,
where everything here is done.

July 2020

ICY BELLOWS

When the snow gathers
heavy and deep,
and the wind rises
from being asleep,

then we know
You have something to say.
That means that You know
there will be no day.

Only an endless night
enclosing us all
as we fall into the pit
where all must fall.

Then the snow mounts
and swirls about us,
taking its time
to fill all means of escape.

Gradually it covers and
     covers,
till all that remains is
its mounting heap.

March 2019

FOR THE WANTING

Yesterday never comes too soon.
Whatever we want, we will always achieve.
Is this what the world teaches us?
Is this what we believe?

By experience I have learnt the contrary.
What I want to do never happens at all.
We learn from our mistakes.
We stumble and fall,
and in the end, learn nothing at all.

Life is a mystery riddled and deep.
It wraps us up tight
and won't let us go.
I have not understood it—
nor has anyone else—
until we enter our final sleep.

October 2014

A PILGRIMAGE

What does it matter what happens tomorrow?
The world turns and twists,
frantically weaving
a garment of truth for a world full of dirt.

Yesterday I discovered the truth.
Now I no longer know what it means.
What I found was a kernel of nothing,
emptying the world of its truth and its bliss.

I darkened the world with a suicide's aim
and ended its pretentions to truth.
I stripped off its robe
and looked underneath,
and found nothing there but a twisted-up mess.

Tell me the truth, Lord,
of a worlding's ravings.
Empty my search for all the wrong things.
Show me what it means
to know You and love You,
and find there the meaning to
        all this.

August 2014

FOUND

After daybreak, the night fell.
Lost in a ditch,
we found you.

Afterwards we came to ourselves
and wondered where you'd been.
But it was grace that found you.

I saw your eyes,
like twinkle toes looking behind you.
Where had you come from?
Where were you going to?
Only God knows.

May 2009

CHRIS AND SAM

Is one like the other?
Or are they quite different.
Only You, the eternal One, knows.
Apparently they don't resemble one another
but who knows what's in their souls.

There is a common denominator in all of us.
So people who seem extremely unalike,
when you come right down to the bottom of it,
are only human beings after all.

Like all of us.

That is why God can love the prince and the pauper.
And that is why we all share a common humanity,
and none of us can look down on one another.
Because only God looks down on us all.

So celebrate our differences and our resemblances.
Come down to us from the author of all.
He is the Source of all our differences,
and He the only One on whom we can call.

That is a truth taking a long time coming
into the vacant spaces of my mind.
Till I finally know what I should always have known—
that we are all one,
one and all.

April 2020

ALL LIFE

Our lives pass by,
imprisoned by time,
which ebbs and flows
like the sea.

We call out for help
from the dark surroundings.
But no one answers or helps.

Lessons in life are bitterly learnt
from the bite of experience's mouth.
Do we have to endure all this?
Is there no way out?

We learn to tolerate things
as we go,
and put up with what we thought we couldn't.
But our Savior guides us all the way
and leads us to a perfect haven.

November 2014

THE OPTIMIST

An eager tomorrow awaits me,
spinning out of time.
Yesterday's shadows encumber it.
They will never fall into line.

But we have a Savior who laughs,
who bids all these things adieu.
They shall never come near us,
hurt us or block out our view.

Let's celebrate this sudden change,
which radiates contentment about us.
Let's walk in it manfully strong
and know that there's nothing wrong.

March 2015

CONTEMPLATIONS

Are we a happy people,
planted here to grow.
From every single nation
in which someone knew the place to go.

This a conundrum within a problem
that makes no sense at all.
Even if we want it to,
it holds us totally enthralled.

"Now isn't that strange" as the poet said
when he stared up into the moon.
There is a world beyond us here,
which we will come to all too soon.

That's it; there isn't anymore to say–
only to give a thousand reasons
why we all forgot to pray.

Please think of me all you way up there
and understand my reasons for daring to disobey.

Then wave me goodbye forever
as I set out on my way.
On my way to find the world,
a world that went away.

February 2020

THE AFTER EIGHT

What is it like to be aboard this vessel of hope
that rounds the world's horns with minimum endeavor
and brings everyone back to their homes.
I was thinking about that as long as forever,
until I could not think anymore.

Then I threw away the pen, wrapped up the book,
and went around the world to explore.
And so I found what it was like to be aboard that great vessel,
breasting the seas unknown.
Tossed about in the wildest of weather
and still finding the path that leads home.

I wish I knew the outcome of all our histories
that follow a path like the ship.
Did they end where they intended,
or did they discover
a way just like that of the ship?

Question and answer,
wrestle and think
with problems that cannot be solved.
And then wish you hadn't even started
on a route beyond reach of this ship.

Because we are men and not ships
bent on a quite different path.
One that can lead to countries strange,
which alter the way we think.

Our journey is quite strange
because other forces are in play
beyond what we ourselves can do.
They shape our paths
and lead us forward
into a fiery furnace
or far, far away.

So we are not free,
or so this poem says.
But creatures of another world
quite different from this.

Because they are playing out their story
in which we only play a part.
And to them, we are quite meaningless,
just icons to be moved round about in play.

Substance and reality, which in fact, are we?
That is an endless story we just started here.

May 2020

THE WAY FORWARD

A field of leaves,
a field of green.
How is life caught betwixt and between?

But I have found on the path of sorrow and dread
that the dead never listen or raise their heads.

But I have found freedom,
a new way forward,
where paths of life commingle and meet.
Such a path should always be taken;
it leads forward and upward to everlasting life.

June 2013

IT ALL WORKS OUT

What do we write about
when the sky fills the air,
and the sun shines endlessly
all day long.

We write about our strivings
and hope to succeed.
And we leave the result
to Him who waters the seed.

I have understood now
that we can't play a game
when it comes to deciding
the fate of our race.

God's purposes are endless,
His purpose eternal,
and all that He's destined
will fall into place.

August 2016

BEFUDDLED

What's life all about?
I wonder and wonder and never find out
because my mind is too small,
while my thoughts are too big.
And to reconcile them together
turns into a gig.

But I have to begin,
or at least make an attempt,
so that I can try to understand
what everybody else has found out.

Just as a beginning has to have an end,
so all the nonsense I give out
should have a meaning
beyond all doubt.

So there you are.
That's the answer to my story—
a puzzle that begins and ends
as I go about.

It doesn't have a meaning.
It doesn't have to have one.
Because it means what the Creator decrees
should be done.

December 2019

ABOUT ME

I wonder about things day after day,
turning pages in my mind.
They reveal nothing that I did not already know,
and in everything I am left far behind.

But thank you, my God, for being my Savior
and leading me out into fields unknown.
Where I can grow and learn and prosper
and find the way back to the fields that were sown.

You have led me all the days of my life.
From beginning to end, it is quite a story,
where sin and destruction thrived and grew.
Regard for You faded,
Your will forgotten
while I sowed a field of thorns of strange hue.

Now I return to serve You anew,
to remember Your Word
and enjoy your delight.
You have found me and blessed me
from now to eternity.
And I know all Your promises will come true.

November 2014

BECOMING FREE

What do I have to say about myself,
a tangled weed that cannot be pulled out?
Many have tried and struggled to free me
but I am forever tied to the ground.

What can we say about God and His Son?
They have wrestled with this problem too.
At first, I thought they would be baffled,
not knowing that they knew a way that is true.

So now, by God's mercy, I am freed from the ground,
free to roam freely wherever I choose.
Always coming back to the One who made me,
who tells me the way I know I should choose.

April 2018

SURRENDER

I want to say something about life,
why I am alive and not dead.
For God has decided these things,
to which we can only concur.

The reason you are living is hidden with God,
and you must accept that you may never know it.
He is the Almighty before time began,
and no one can gainsay His rule.

What He has decided will certainly happen,
and only a fool would disagree.
Amen and Amen the angels say
and there's nothing more to say.

But then again, everything has a purpose and meaning,
though we may never know what they are.
But it is about our living and the way we do it,
and how God tells us to go.

If we follow the Lord and listen to His voice,
we will understand what to do.
And our lives, under His guidance,
will lead to an ending that is true.

August 2020

AN UNFINISHED JOURNEY

Are we together again
as we were in the past?
Or is this part of a new beginning,
far away from the past?

The past reaches out, not wanting to let go
of its hold on all the victims it's slain.
It will not relinquish its powerful grasp
until we tell it to go.

We are the authors of our own salvation;
it is we who determines its course.
Whether onward into Satan's outstretched arms
or far away from the curse.

I have tried it,
so I know what it means
        to be free.

Away from the deep dungeon
He holds us in
and into our Savior's arms.
There we can feel
what new freedom is like
and begin our journey home.

A journey in which there are new things to discover
and a new way to lead a new life.

Hallelujah for this glorious outcome
of everything that went before.
And we pray,
God will hold us
to this course going forward,
to become what He wants us to be.

May 2020

GOING HOME

Today I saw the sunset.
I heard its whispered voice.
I love it for its colors.
I bless it for its choice.

I will not always look on it.
I will not often hear it tell
of time that has been past,
of roads I know so well.

Those yesterdays are now forgot;
those pathways are now trod.
A new way dawns before me,
a new way home to God.

September 2014

FORTITUDE

I will bear the blows of fortune.
I will take what heaven sends.
I will wend my way through life
till I reach the end of ends.

Tomorrow will rise sun-blest,
all those yesterdays forgot.
What has been will be no more,
what was then and what was not.

I will stride the path of hope
till at last it leads me home.
I will know the fortune finished,
time at last I cease to roam.

That will be a day of glory.
That will be a day of hope.
That will end my endless story.
That will break the final rope.

April 2005

Printed in the United States
By Bookmasters